A Guide to Help Teenagers Against Self Harm

Table of Contents

Introduction.....3
Chapter 1: Teenage Self-Injury....6
Chapter 2: Assist your child lessen self-injurious behavior....14
Chapter 3: Immediate Strategies for Parents when Teenager self-harms....19
Chapter 4: Approach to assistance when teenager self-harms....27
Chapter 5: Ways to Assist Teens Who Self-Harm.....42
Conclusion.....49

Introduction

I want to thank you and congratulate you for downloading the book, A Guide to Help Teenagers Against Self Harm

Self-injury is a term utilized when somebody harms or injures himself or herself intentionally as opposed to coincidentally. Usual instances are cutting, hitting, scratching or smoldering. Endeavored self-killing is the most serious type of self-harm. For some, self-injury is seen as a sign of escaping from a situation. It is not utilized as a method for murdering oneself. The strategy used to self-injure can convey dangers, and in spite of the fact that the expectation may not be there, there might be grave repercussions. For other individuals, the expectation behind self-injury will be to killing themselves. These are clinically depressed individuals. Musings about suicide can be basic in teenagers who are clinically depressed. These could be latent considerations to dynamic musings.

Sadness is a disease - it is not a condition where you can get a hold of yourself. While nervousness can instigate self-hurt in a few, anxiety or feeling stressed out is likewise associated with sadness, since it regularly happens before somebody gets depressed. As tension expands so does the chances of despondency. This is roundabout – as clinical depression expands the sentiments of nervousness, which in turn elevates the emotions of stress, rumination, obsessive state of mind.

Anxiety is the most well-known feeling we encounter and the most well-known type of turmoil in youth and in grown-up individuals. At some point in life everybody will feel on edge when confronted with troublesome or new circumstances. Everybody can identify with manifestations of uneasiness or dread and experience side effects like breathing getting to be shallow, perspiration, tachycardia, butterflies in their stomach, and dry mouth. For a better insight into self-harm, methods to prevent, and steps to alleviate, read on....

Chapter 1: Teenage Self-Injury

By definition, self-injury alludes to harming oneself to diminish feelings of torment or misery. The most well-known types of this conduct are cutting and burning. The least popular variations of self-injury are drawing out clumps of hairs, hitting the dividers, and consuming harmful substances or piercing with sharp objects.

Numerous teenagers today are attempting to manage harsh levels of anxiety in school, in their families, and in their associate connections. Some of these teenagers are over-scheduled and being rushed through their teenage years by parents and companions alike. Teenagers have gotten to be helpless prey to our very dangerous, media-driven world. Being before a PC or watching TV for several hours a day has become a common business and more vital than spending quality time with family and companions. Youthful young ladies are continually being shelled by pictures in the media about how they ought to look and act. Particularly for teenage girls, inability to experience these admired pictures can lead to binge eating and/or participating in self-injury conduct as a type of self-discipline.

Causes of Teenager Self-injurious behavior

Like substance misuse, teenagers self-harming conduct encompasses over all social and financial levels. We do know that more teenage females take part in this conduct than teen males and that self-harming teenagers are seldom self-destructive. The greater part of these teenagers are looking for swift alleviation from feelings of misery.

One noteworthy motivation behind why teenagers float towards self-harming practices is the endorphin impact. When teenagers cut or smolder themselves, endorphins are immediately rushed into their circulation systems and they encounter a desensitizing or pleasurable sensation. For some of these teenagers, cutting or burning themselves paralyses the disagreeable musings and sentiments. Like dependence on a specific medication, the endorphin gives quick acting help to teenagers from their emotional misery and numerous stressors in their lives.

Other significant reasons with reference to why teenagers take part in self-harm include:

- Feeling clearly disengaged from or discredited by their folks.

- Wanting to harmonize inside a specific associate gathering that supports and remunerates self-harming conduct.

- Feeling clearly dead inside or feeling undetectable in their folks' eyes. Self-harm makes them feel invigorated inside and affirms their presence as a general rule.

- For teenage girls, self-injury might be utilized as an adapting system to excessively demanding parents, particularly in circumstances where the father is the overwhelming with regards to control and deciding.

Opportune time to Seek Assistance

Since teenagers frequently participate in self-harming practices secretly or with their companions, parents may not know that this issue exists. Likewise, parents additionally should know that there is a major distinction between self-adorning and self-harming conduct.

It is a well known prevailing fashion among teenagers today to body piercing and tattoo as a type of self-adorning. Teenagers who self-harm are looking for help from emotional misery, they are not self-adorning.

Here are some signs that may demonstrate that a teenager has an issue with self-harming conduct:

- Cut or burn blemishes on their arms, legs, and abdomen.

- Finding blades, extremely sharp objects, cutters, and other sharp articles covered up in the teenager's room.

- Regularly bolting herself or himself up in the room or restroom after an awful day at school, negative experiences with associates, and family clashes for protracted time periods.

- The family doctor, an educator, or other grown-up watches bruises, or that the teenager seems to be frequently expelling real hairs.

- The teenager's companions cut or smolder themselves.

- Reports from a kin showing that he or she discovered blood stained razors or observed the teenager in the demonstration of self-harming

Treatments that work

By a wide margin, the best treatment for juvenile self-harming issues is family treatment. A talented family specialist will have the capacity to enhance family communication, and educate on conflict resolution between parents and teenagers.

Expertise building gatherings can be useful to self-harming teenagers also. A decent gathering ought to educate teenagers successful tools for dealing with their temperaments, tackle unhelpful musings, perception and meditation aptitudes, and sound exercises to better supervise stress.

Means of preventing teenager self-injury

Parents assume a vital role in keeping their teenagers from taking part in self-harming practices and from joining an undesirable associate gathering, where this issue might be the glue that binds them together. At home, parents can organize get together as a family. Parents can put the teenager responsible for selecting and arranging a weekend outing for the family. The family disposition should be more quiet and welcoming for the teenager. When clashes do erupt or crises happen, relatives ought to cooperate as a group to bring about solutions. Teenagers need to find a place in the hearts and minds of their folks. They have to feel acknowledged and realize that their folks will be there for them unequivocally. It is the parents' obligation to make firm limits between their work and family lives.

One approach to cultivate more significant associations among parents and teenagers is to share family stories. Parents ought to express to their children what their battles and high focuses were in their lives. They can likewise express to their teenagers any critical, useful tidbits and stories that their own particular parents expressed to them when they were growing up.

Self-harming conduct can be perilous, especially if the teenager is misusing liquor and different medications. Parents need to take a firm position and set reliable cutoff points with these practices. Parents additionally need to educate on their teenagers' consumption limits of liquor and solid approaches to supervise stress.

It is a parent's entitlement to meet their teenager's companions, and in addition their folks, and voice your worries when justified.

Should a parent find that their teenager is participating in hazardous and risky conduct, for example, self-harm, they ought to be assured that a family therapist will have the capacity to skillfully help the family and teenager with this major issue.

Chapter 2: Assist your child lessen self-injurious behavior

Self-harm or perpetrating physical misuse onto one's body to ease feelings of distress is not unusual in children and teenagers. There are numerous types of self-injury, including cutting, scratching, hitting, and smoldering. Numerous children and teenagers who self-harm likewise battle with melancholy, nervousness, dietary issues, physical misuse or different genuine concerns or cognitive issues.

These teenagers do not know how to verbalize their emotions, and rather, act them by self-harming. Teenagers may self-harm to alleviate profound melancholy or other overpowering feelings. They may do it to communicate abhorrence or disgrace. They may do it to express negative contemplations they cannot express. They may do it since they feel powerless.

Studies have found that self-harm is an addictive conduct. Clinical studies interface the use of sedatives. When a kid self-hurts, the endorphins surge the circulation system. The surge is pleasing to the point that a kid figures out how to partner self-hurt as alleviating, rather than being ruinous.

Self-injury is called non-suicidal self-injury (NSSI) on the grounds that there is no expectation to commit suicide, however, self-injury can prompt conscious suicide.

In the event that you observe symptoms of self-injury, take your teenager to a therapist for an expert assessment. A therapist will figure out if self-injury is self-destructive or non-self-destructive by performing a suicide appraisal (and discover if different concerns are existing). They will likewise educate your teenager procedures for managing difficult feelings or circumstances.

Besides taking your teenager to a therapist, there are different ways you can help them diminish the inclination to self-injury:

1. Make an improvised unit.

Keep positive and mood elevating items in a box or a container, which your teenager can utilize when they get the feelings to self-harm. This can be anything from a diary to artwork supplies to perky music to photographs of companions, family or their legends. Add anything your teenager may observe as quieting or encouraging.

2. Model positive symbolism

Envisioning a lovely, quiet place is an incredible approach to lessen tension or agonizing feelings. When you hone positive symbolism before your kid you help them reinforce these abilities. Talking resoundingly as you depict a mitigating scene – like a shoreline – or positive recollections of a spot you have been to and utilizing distinctive subtle elements in your portrayals too might help.

3. Discuss triggers.

Help your teenager better comprehend the sorts of circumstances and stressors that trigger their negative emotions. If there is a test coming up in school or a dental specialist visit, discuss how the days ahead can be taxing. This helps your teenager be fully aware and have the fundamental aptitudes available to them. Likewise, discuss your own triggers and the solid ways you adapt.

4. Recommend utilizing less serious practices.

If the desire to self-harm is still present utilizing less serious activities, for example, holding an ice cube, tearing paper, destroying a sheet, snapping an elastic band, sucking a lemon peel and beating a pillow might help.

5. Recommend participating in physical exercises.

The surge of adrenaline in physical activities, for example, running, moving and playing chase with their pet, really creates the same compound surge that self-harming does. Therefore, try to engage your teenager in as much physical activities as possible.

6. Be sympathetic about misfortunes.

Curtailing self-harming conduct is not simple, and it will require some serious energy. Your teenager may have misfortunes. The best approach, if a mishap happens, is to offer nonjudgmental backing. Studies demonstrate that disgrace, feedback, or reaction when parents see an injury causes kids to pull back once more into self-harming practices.

Once more, in the event that you think your teenager is self-hurting, make a meeting with a therapist for an appraisal and bolster them in honing solid adapting methodologies.

Overcoming self-harm is not simple, however, with successful mediation, your teenager can prevent these practices and show signs of improvement. The key is to get help.

Chapter 3: Immediate Strategies for Parents when Teenager self-harms

If you have a high school child or little girl, you may have heard the expression self-harm whispered in quiet tones by another parent or an educator. Some individuals think it is only a pattern which is not to be considered excessively important. Yet, studies recommends that self-harm is an undeniable and progressing development. Also, considering that self-injury is one of the greatest indicators of teenage suicide, it is unquestionably not an issue to hide.

For parents, it can be extremely hard to comprehend where this sort of conduct originates from. Actually, it is presumably not something you would have even found out about when you were growing up.

Read on to discover answers to basic queries concerning self-harm and some viable guidance about what to do if your kid is self-hurting.

Meaning of self-harm

Self-harm (also called self-injury) can portray a scope of strategies to hurt oneself physically. It can incorporate the following:

- Cutting, scratching, picking or scratching the skin;
- Plucking out one's own hair;
- Scalding one's own skin;
- Ingesting toxic substances; and,
- Bone wounding or breaking.

Needs for a youngster to self-harm

- The reasons why any individual may participate in self-harm can differ broadly. For a few, it might be an enthusiastic or addictive custom that they perform paying little heed to how their life is going. Others may just self-hurt amid times of high stress or after a traumatic episode.

- Following are the reasons why teenagers may self-hurt:

- Some teenagers report that the physical torment they encounter while hurting themselves can serve to dull the emotional torment.

- When a teenager self-hurts in a formal way they may feel it quiets them down or to feel just as they have a feeling of control over circumstances throughout their life.

- Self-despise and venting of resentment towards oneself can likewise bring about self-harmful conduct.

- Other young people report that self-hurting can afford them a heightened feeling or experience. Such individuals report that they cannot feel things or that they feel flat. They may contend that self-harm strengthens their encounters and permits them to quickly escape from the triviality of their life.

The most well-known misguided judgment about self-injury is that it is just an attention-seeking conduct. This is usually not the situation. The reality of the matter is that some individuals self-harm trying to apply some level of control over others to exert some kind of pressure.

Self-harm may give impermanent alleviation to the individual, however, it does not help them manage fundamental issues. In the long haul, numerous individuals who self-harm may wind up with lasting scars and have a tendency to heighten the self-harm after some time.

Teenagers with a current anxiety issues, dietary problem or depression are the most at the danger of participating in self-injury and they should be educated on methodologies to supplant the negative adapting conduct to more positive choices.

Self-harm is profoundly related with suicide, yet there is an unmistakable differentiation between the individuals who expect to self-hurt for the reasons outlined above and the individuals who truly wish to end their own lives.

The issues that lead a teenager to self-harm furthermore lead a teenager to endeavor suicide are frequently related, yet the thinking behind self-harm and suicide endeavors are entirely diverse.

Steps to follow when teenager self-harms

If you find your teenager has self-harmed here are some key steps to follow:

1. In the event that the wounds are not deep, it is essential to instantly counsel a medical practitioner, the emergency department of your neighborhood hospital or a psychological well-being professional.

2. Try not to go overboard to any proof of self-harm, for example, scars or smolders. Be practical.

3. Dress the injuries in the event that they are still recent or give proper emergency treatment.

4. Pose some questions:

- How did it happen? Approach the event step-by-step.

- What instrument was used to perpetrate the self-harm?

- Where was the location of the incident?

- How would they say they were feeling at the time?

- What contemplations they were experiencing their mind?

- Have they self-harmed some time recently? Assuming this is the case, how frequently? Keep in mind to approach this as a chance for open exchange to give your teenager a chance to let you know how they are feeling.

5. Consider: What do you think they require from you at this moment?

6. Decide the seriousness of the self-injury, (e.g., are the cuts shallow or profound?)

7. Look for expert help. An accomplished child psychologist can recognize the fundamental issues that might add to the self-hurt and will help your teenager to create elective adapting techniques to supplant the negative method for dealing with stress of self-harm.

8. Execute a security arrangement at home:

- Remove perilous items.
- Ensure the teenager is not left alone (particularly in the bathroom or bedroom) with the entryway shut.

- Check in with them consistently to perceive how they are doing.

9. Actualize a security arrangement at school:

- If conceivable, pick up your teenager from school or organize a trusted individual to pick them up. Try not to leave them at home alone.

- Talk to pertinent staff (on a 'need-to-know' basis) and ensure everybody is in agreement. Advise staff about symptoms to look for.

- Ask the school to expel hazardous items where conceivable.

- Ensure that their teenagers are not left alone in anyplace, (for example, the bathrooms or change rooms).

Chapter 4: Approach to assistance when teenager self-harms

Consistently, pediatricians treat with care the teenagers who hurt themselves intentionally, in ways that include cutting, smoldering, scraping, and hitting. About 1 in 6 young people has attempted self-harm at any rate once. Clinicians and scientists accordingly frequently discuss this as non-suicidal self-injury.

A pediatrician is likely the principal clinician to find that the teenager has been self-hurting. Wounds or scars might be revealed amid a routine physical examination or a terrified parent may require a pressing assessment of a teenager. The main clinical experience can be troublesome for everybody: Parents regularly encounter blame, treachery, or shock; the teenager may feel uncovered and embarrassed; the pediatrician may react with disappointment or just incomprehension. The main clinical experience is likewise basic for setting the phase for fruitful treatment.

The objective of this article is to present the occurrence of non-suicidal self-injury, including data on who self-harms and why. Regarding treatment, an assortment of compelling and proof based mediations for self-harm are accessible, yet most require special training and are actualized over a protracted time frame. Therefore, this discourse concentrates on the preparatory assessment of non-suicidal self-injury with an accentuation for essential consideration for primary care doctors on the best way to display a steady and nonjudgmental position that can encourage further evaluation.

Why self-harm?

It is natural to group self-injury as an issue and to accept that once the conduct has halted the patient will feel better. In any case, studies demonstrate that the most widely recognized capacity of self-harm is to deal with a scope of negative feelings or to make feeling where there is just lifelessness or emptiness. The issue for the patient is feeling unendurably dismal, on edge, embarrassed, or forlorn—or not feeling anything by any means. Self-injury is an answer that, in the short term, can be staggeringly powerful at facilitating insufferable feelings.

In this circumstance, non-suicidal self-injury gives alleviation instantly and freely of any reaction from the outside world. Young people do not begin self-harming just to get consideration. Indeed, numerous teenagers self-harm in isolation for quite a long time or years before they are found, and as opposed to looking for consideration will find a way to conceal their conduct. Once found, the conduct can be a radical new dimension. Contingent upon the response they get from people around them, teenagers who have couple of passionate abilities may rapidly figure out how to utilize non-suicidal self-injury as an approach to influence others.

For instance, if a teenager begins cutting herself since she feels forlorn and cannot endure it, and her family reacts by hurrying to express love and bolster, it is likely that she will begin harming herself each time she needs fondness. Alternately, if a teenager is hopeless at school and is permitted to stay home each time he begins hitting himself, he may keep hitting himself at whatever point things get especially strained at school. Of course, then, teenagers in group tests report utilizing non-suicidal self-injury as a method for affecting individuals and of imparting distress.

As these cases propose, non-suicidal self-injury can work to abstain from something unsavory or to incite a response, regardless of the fact that it is a negative one. In this manner, numerous experts may reject teenagers who self-harm as manipulative. In any case, it is ordinary to need consideration. Everybody tries to minimize enduring and to expand delight. The issue is that the self-injuring teenagers may not know how to request help in an immediate or viable way. Self-injury is a provisional and botching answer for an inability to convey or to have basic needs met.

A long way from being the expert controllers that some may make them out to be, teenagers who cut or hit themselves are frequently attempting to deal with their feelings and their connections without truly knowing how. Basically, in our experience, numerous teenagers who self-harm do as such on the grounds that they do not realize what else to do. This is an imperative foundation of a significant number of the medications for non-suicidal self-injury, which intend to educate elective critical thinking techniques.

Who self-harms

Taking into account the clarifications we have offered, teenagers use non-suicidal self-injury to oversee negative or discharge emotions and to impart enduring when they do not have the capacity to apply more compelling arrangements. Accordingly, it augurs well that rates of self-harm are most astounding in those with alarming feelings, mind boggling or stormy connections, and poor adapting skills.

Non-suicidal self-injury in teenagers was viewed as a marker of serious and conceivably long lasting sickness. In any case, studies propose that non-suicidal self-injury frequently happens autonomously of border personality disorder, especially in patients with sorrow or substance misuse or even in those with no other diagnosable psychopathology.

Appraisals of the predominance of self-harm differ as indicated by evaluation philosophy and by regardless of whether nonfatal suicide endeavors are incorporated into the tally. However, self-injury is acknowledged to be particularly regular in teenagers. Although non-suicidal self-injury has been generally connected with young girls and ladies, all the more as of late studies recommend there may not be a gender orientation distinction in existence.

Non-suicidal self-injury and suicide

By definition, non-suicidal self-injury is self-harm inflicted without the desire to end the life. Individuals who take part in this sort of self-harm are not showing self-destructive conduct. Despite what might be expected, they frequently utilize non-suicidal self-injury as an approach to make being alive more endurable. In any case, non-suicidal self-injury is a risk factor for later suicide endeavors.

People who take part in non-suicidal self-injury will probably consider suicide and to really endeavor executing themselves. Non-suicidal self-injury that happens more often and in more serious structures is likewise a solid indicator of self-destructive conduct. In a clinical example of discouraged teenagers, non-suicidal self-injury anticipated future suicide endeavors pretty much as emphatically as past suicide attempts. This connection between non-suicidal self-injury and suicide held up when the analysts controlled for demographic contrasts, psycho-social conditions, and comorbid psychopathologies.

It is still indistinct whether non-suicidal self-injury drives specifically to self-destructive conduct or if agonizing sentiments lead to both. In any case, teenagers who participate in non-suicidal self-injury ought to be surveyed for quick suicide hazard as a major aspect of their clinical assessment, regardless of the possibility that suicide is not inexorably the sole or focal core interest.

Assessing Non-suicidal Self-injury

While assessing a teenager who participates in non-suicidal self-injury, it is imperative to first build up a general association with the teenager by getting some information about school, home life, kinships, and activities At that point, a pediatrician can steer into getting some information about non-suicidal self-injury. A decent first question is whether the self-harm helped in any way. This is the same as just asking the reasons for self-harm, however, the previous query is less inclined to be seen as accusatory. Stated along these lines, the inquiry exhibits a comprehension of the utilization of non-suicidal self-injury as an answer. Essentially, it can lead to paving the way to a more particular discourse of psychiatric side effects (despondency, indignation, uneasiness) and interpersonal stressors (strained associations with parents, breakups, loss of companionships).

Another methodology is to request that the patient recall a particular example of self-harm. Supportive inquiries can include: any recollections of the feelings before the self-harm, any changes in those feelings after the self-harm, and the way it felt at the time of self-harm. Try to be nonjudgmental and safe.

Next, a child specialist ought to attempt to pick up data on the teenager's state of mind and the logistics of self-harm. His queries can be modeled as follows: the way the self-harm was carried out, instruments that were utilized, frequency of self-harm, and the areas of the body involved in self-harm.

The specialist ought to likewise give real therapeutic data that can minimize difficulties and extra damage. For instance, doctors can guide patients about the dangers of blood-borne diseases and guarantee tetanus inoculations are updated.

Self-harm is an indication that a teenager is encountering both uncomfortable emotions and is poorly prepared to manage them. Along these lines, the general expert ought to get some information about different perilous practices that, similar to self-harm, have a tendency to be utilized to manage stress. Disorderly eating, substance misuse, and dangerous sexual movement are all connected with self-harm and can have autonomous restorative results that warrant evaluation. Normalizing the experience can help teenagers discuss practices that they accept may cause them harm. Queries can be: whether the teenager was feeling better about something that might be dangerous in the long run, or was the stress so bad that is driving the teenager to abuse drugs or alcohol as an attempt to get away.

Of note, albeit numerous experts used to underestimate that teenagers who take part in non-suicidal self-injury had encountered childhood abuse, studies have demonstrated that the relationship is considerably more modest. Many who have been abused do not go ahead to self-harm and numerous who self-harmed have never been abused. Abuse happens, both inside and outside the home, and the workplace of a trusted medical specialist might be a decent place to discuss it. An accommodating first approach is to find out if an earlier physical or mental abuse is still affecting the teenager. In addition to abuse, the doctor should also screen the teenager for episodes of bullying, which is regularly disregarded and can be serious.

At last, in spite of the fact that we have demonstrated that non-suicidal self-injury ought not to be perplexed with self-destructive conduct, it is critical to assess for suicide hazard.

This is a zone where it is useful to be matter-of-fact, with movement from the general to the specific questioning: are the things so terrible that you thought you are better off dead, whether the teenager had contemplated about self-murder, whether there are any plans to consider murdering yourself now.

For building a collusion and of doing a complete assessment, it is vital to likewise approach about what is going admirably for the teenager. Is there a companion who is especially encouraging? Is there a class at which the teenager does well? Does the patient have an imaginative or musical ability? These connections and aptitudes are the premise for some level of self-regard. They can be attracted on treatment to help the teenager to show signs of improvement and to give a photo of somebody who is more than only a self-injurer.

Secrecy

Numerous teenagers will inquire as to whether what they reveal can be kept in confidence. In spite of the fact that discussions between doctors and their patients are by and large classified, when well-being is in question a patient's folks should be educated. On account of non-suicidal self-injury, this implies the response to that question is frequently 'no.' It is essential to disclose to teenagers that their well-being is their essential concern and that they will do what it takes to safeguard it.

You can offer to help them enlighten their folks concerning the issue, and to intercede what is liable to be a candidly charged discussion. You can likewise guarantee them that you would not converse with their folks without their consent. It is vital that parents or legitimate guardians be educated with the goal that they can bolster and take part in treatment.

Most adolescents who are discussing non-suicidal self-injury interestingly are leaving on a journey including numerous experiences with medical professionals. It might be convenient in the short term, however, it is definitely harming in the long haul to guarantee privacy that you cannot or ought not to convey.

Psychopharmacologic treatment

As of now, there is no endorsed medical solution for the particular treatment of non-suicidal self-injury. Patients who experience the ill effects of sadness and/or nervousness may profit by the medicines of those conditions. Scientists have additionally recommended that non-suicidal self-injury attempts to control negative feelings by means of the endogenous opioid system. Medicine is not considered as a treatment for non-suicidal self-injury.

Psychotherapy

Distinctive sorts of therapy for the treatment of non-suicidal self-injury have in like manner the need for steady helpful contact for a generally long time. For all intents and purposes, a teenager who self-harms warrants a referral to a psychological wellness specialist. How and with what earnestness the referral is made relies on upon the risk of the specific patient being referred to. Teenagers, who are more delicate, more separated, less fruitful, and who have families with limited resources will require referral more desperately to a psychological well-being clinician than other people who are not at such high hazard.

Any patient who is at unavoidable danger for suicide ought to be assessed quickly by an emergency group or in a crisis office.

He or she may require inpatient hospitalization to guarantee well-being in the short term. The inpatient group ought to then help the specialist and the family in building up longer-term outpatient psychological wellness care.

Chapter 5: Ways to Assist Teens Who Self-Harm

My sharp-edged instrument was made from a case cutter, effectively masked in my sack of school tools. I took the sharp-edged instrument and cut another slice profound over my wrist. I fought the desire to cut along the way of my veins. I knew if I did, that would be my last demonstration. I had gained from a companion that cutting along the width of my wrist would just make a scar, an indication of my torment, however, that a cut up my arm would likely end my life. Furthermore, I was not there. However, I knew I would not like to live in torment any longer, however, I additionally realized that I would not like to pressurize my folks with my torment. Furthermore, to be perfectly honest, I did not know whether they would get it. All the more significantly, I did not need the judgment, the inquiries, and the fake sensitivity that would likely happen after the discussion. In my teenaged personality, the main thing that seemed well and good was to endure the horrifying days, weeks, months, and years of steady recollections or to figure out how to anesthetize those rehashed, terrible minutes again and again, trusting they would blur into blankness.

Furthermore, my folks never knew. I had figured out how to conceal my agony and yearning to just desert everything by wearing since a long time ago sleeved shirts. My updates were still there, only a slender layer of fabric over my tissue. Also, when cutting no more gave that get away, I played with pills. Anything accessible in the bureau, I attempted. Dull days were both behind and before me.

I no more trusted family, companions, or officials. I hurt for somebody to solace me and improve things.

However, without anybody knowing, I could never escape this dull spot. It is just by the finesse of a cherishing God that I am still here to share my story. He thoughtfully brought me through an extra seven years to the date of my salvation that would change everything.

As I think back in the course of the last a quarter century, I realize that I have taken in a considerable measure. As a parent now, I might want to share eleven perceptions and considerations that may help you if you have a youngster who is enduring an agony so profound that they feel a need to cut, cure, or even longing to confer suicide:

1. Prevent free thinking and conformism in family. Stay away from radicalism and legalism in your family. Your youngster will see both as a need to revolt, detecting no elegance and chance to talk and share his fears and concerns.

2. Make a domain that is inviting. Make a situation that is inviting, not judging when a kid accompanies a mystery or an ardent need. Once more, the kid needs to feel that the most secure spot to talk is at home.

3. Find out if parents are making it difficult to converse with you. Tell the kid that if they are ever excessively uncomfortable, making it impossible to converse with you that they ought to converse with a grown-up companion who can hand-off the data to you. Regularly, the kid fears offending the parent and will save the parent over uncovering their own torment. Youngsters have a characteristic yearning to secure their folks.

4. Look out for the usual symptoms. Watch out for the indications of young dejection, including the accompanying:

- Feeling consistently dismal or blue.

- Talking about suicide or being ideally dead.

- Becoming all of a sudden a great deal more touchy.

- Having a deterioration in school or home activities.

- Reporting constant physical objections and/or making numerous visits to class medical caretakers.

- Failing to take part in previously pleasurable activities or associations with companions.

- Abusing substances.

5. Prevent offering numerous answers for their issues. Abstain from offering excessively numerous answers for their issues. Teenagers are just yearning to be listened. Ensure your teenager realizes that you will offer scriptural astuteness when they inquire.

6. Listen to the music that your teenager listens to. Listen to the music that your teenager listens to. You can regularly decide their mind-set or outlook through the words and hints of their playlist.

7. Go off with your teen in a fun excursion. Give time to escape with your teenager in a fun situation. Make recollections that are pleasant. In the moment of joy, a teenager may feel the flexibility to open up.

8. Be open for discussion. Talk at extremely inconvenient times of the night. Because of the physical changes, melatonin is discharged about two hours for teenagers. Their heart windows are regularly more open between 10 p.m. until 1 a.m.

9. Share your own past issues with your teenager. Share your own particular past damages and battles with your teenagers. You have a story, and they have to realize that. We regularly conceal our pasts from our youngsters to ensure them or so they do not consider gravely of us.

10. Seek counseling if the sadness persists. Try not to be reluctant to look for counseling if the melancholy proceeds. Nouthetic counseling locations the battles from a scriptural point of view. There are likewise other incredible alternatives that can be offered through your congregation. Never be hesitant to look for help. It does not imply that you are a disappointment as a parent. Truth be told, it implies that you adore your kid and longing the best for them.

11. Supplicate. Try not to think little of the force of supplication. Implore with and for your teenager. Give them a chance to hear your heart cry with them. Furthermore, supplicate some more.

Conclusion

Thank you again for downloading this book, How to Train Teenagers against Self Harm

The objective of the pediatrician's consideration is to set up a protected specialist-patient relationship, which will help the patient acknowledge benefits and take an interest effectively in treatment. Given the irritating way of self-harm and the continuous supposition that the individuals who self-harm are simply controlling people around them, it can be troublesome for the pediatrician to come to the respectful and nonjudgmental position that is best in building a protected, trusting relationship. A superior comprehension of why teenagers self-harm and what should be possible to help them show signs of improvement is an initial phase in making an agreeable, sympathetic relationship. This work is troublesome—yet remunerating.

Finally, if you enjoyed this book, please take the time to share your thoughts and post a review on Amazon. It would be greatly appreciated!

Thank you and good luck!